Moving on into Morning

Also by Elsie Wear Stockwell

The Light Between the Leaves

For a Stranger Here

Moving on into Morning

Narrative by
James T. Stockwell

Poems and Illustrations by
Elsie Wear Stockwell

iUniverse, Inc.
New York   Bloomington

Moving On Into Morning

iUniverse books may be ordered through booksellers or by contacting:

iUniverse
1663 Liberty Drive
Bloomington, IN 47403
www.iuniverse.com
1-800-Authors (1-800-288-4677)

Because of the dynamic nature of the Internet, any Web addresses or links contained in this book may have changed since publication and may no longer be valid.

ISBN: 978-1-4401-2133-3 (pbk)
ISBN: 978-1-4401-2134-0 (ebk)

Library of Congress Control Number: 2009924628

Printed in the United States of America

iUniverse rev. date: 3/30/2009

Bonnie Stockwell and Rhoda Stockwell provided invaluable assistance in the preparation of *Moving on into Morning*.

In Memory of My Wife

Contents

List of Illustrations

Foreword

The second opinion confirmed the first diagnosis: fourth-stage lung cancer; six months to live without treatment, six months to three years with treatment, depending upon the efficacy of the drugs, which were now in trial stages. Life had taken on a new meaning for my seventy-year-old bride of fifty-one years, who paid meticulous attention to her diet, preferred being a vegetarian, and maintained her body weight at fit and trim levels. Although she had had a mastectomy two years earlier, cancer cells found their way into a most vulnerable part of her body.

Elsie was a creative person who took pride in her accomplishments and appearance. While she struggled with cancer, I reverted to disciplines and procedures that had served me so well in the past, such as keeping a daily journal, updating our appointment calendar, planning ahead, and communicating with family. As much as I tried to take control, cancer had a routine of its own and took away Elsie eighteen months after the first signs of the disease appeared. In looking back, I found that turning the journal into a narrative and combining it with poems that she had written about her experience presented a compelling picture of two persons facing death. I am now better prepared to accept those situations that cannot be controlled and will be grateful to her forever for poems that present insight for me and for others who will ultimately live out their last days.

Elsie grew up in a privileged household with a dominant mother. Perhaps their frequent clashes led to her mother's approval of her oldest daughter's marriage two weeks after she turned nineteen. Before eight years had gone by, there were five children aged six and under, and I was keeping irregular hours as a partner in a 1957 high-tech startup. We had no full-time help, and Elsie filled the shoes of both mother and father for the children. If that wasn't enough pressure, I was diagnosed with multiple sclerosis before she turned thirty, and she had to face the prospect of bringing up five children with a physically and emotionally challenged husband.

The MS diagnosis had a huge impact on our lives. The diagnostic tools available in the early sixties were limited to eye and physical examinations, and the prognosis for all new patients was discouraging. The doctors advised us to plan for one year, before I became completely incapacitated or died. At the time of my diagnosis, our fears were fueled by the news that one of my first cousins had MS; unfortunately, she died a few years later. In response to my diagnosis, I built a go-it-alone wall around myself, seriously impairing my communication with Elsie and cutting the bonds of love and friendship with children, friends, and other family members. I rationalized that it was my problem to deal with, not the rest of the world's.

Before my diagnosis, Elsie and I were very close, shared all of our hopes and doubts, and felt free to aggressively argue both minor and major issues. After the diagnosis, Elsie felt frozen out and overwhelmed by my illness. She thought that she would have to raise the children alone and face the economic consequences brought on by an unemployed husband. The trust that had been built between us during the first ten years of our marriage was shattered. She lost her focus, kept to herself, and watched with apprehension as I struggled, trying to keep up a good front while suffering the initial physical impacts of MS on my body.

Even though Elsie was devastated, she forced herself to prepare for the future by earning her real estate license and applying for a job. She was offered an entry-level position in a shabby office in an industrial location. I expressed my concern about her safety, and I told her that somehow we could find a way to make ends meet. We both became active in ATOMS (Association to Overcome Multiple Sclerosis). We attended monthly meetings, often with kids in tow. They were living with a mom and dad who were just as scared as they were. We hoped that by exposing them to other patients and their families they might more easily make the transition to my departure.

Miraculously, within a year I went into remission, with only minor physical aftereffects, and I was able to continue my leadership position in the high-tech startup. However, the high-tech world of the sixties brought and then took away millions, and we had to adjust our lifestyle to fit the economic consequences. The steps included sale of our summer home, sale of our principal residence in Cambridge, and a total makeover of our spending habits. At our lowest point, we shared a two-bedroom apartment, dog and all, with our youngest daughter in a three-flight walk-up near Tufts University, where she was a student.

Elsie was built for challenge: she was courageous, dedicated, demanding, intellectually curious, highly focused, and she had a strong will. As our children reached high school age, she found her own voice again and pursued her talents as a poet and artist. She became a published author, wrote more than ten thousand poems, and produced hundreds of impressionistic pastels and oils during her lifetime.

This book is focused on the last eighteen months of her life. She continued to write poetry until several weeks before she died, but did not have a chance to edit the poems, and I didn't read them until about a year after she died. When I did go over them, I heard her voice again and was struck by the emotions of two voices: the patient and the partner, facing unknowns. In *Moving on into Morning* her poems from this period are interwoven with some of her earlier poems. My narrative provides the key dates and technical details and reveals my emotions while I faced the loss of my wife, best friend, and partner of fifty-two years. In her poems she talks with candor, sometimes with humor, about her earlier life, her doctors and hospital visits, the progress of her disease—and she gives us her innermost feelings as death approaches.

We had always felt secure living in the Boston area, where we had access to some of the best doctors and hospitals in the world. In spite of our hopes and prayers, the sands gradually began to erode under our feet. Over the course of eighteen months, we learned that although there are some miracles, most fourth-stage lung cancer patients do not survive. However, this book presents a story of survival: the writings of a poet and illustrations of an artist. Together, our voices tell a story of hope and despair that challenged our love for life and our love for each other.

The following narrative presents my recollection of the events that transpired during the last eighteen months of Elsie's life. Some of my memories may have been blurred or embellished by time. The narrative is broken into sections that match the chapters of poems that follow. I chose this structure to give a reader the option of reading the narrative and the poems without interruption or coupling the narrative sections with the related chapters of poems. The content of some of the poems may be more easily understood using the second option.

Breathing Problems

In January of 2002 Elsie had a radical mastectomy at the New England Baptist Hospital. She did not seem to suffer any annoying side effects, but in the spring of 2003 she was experiencing some minor breathing problems and shortness of breath. She felt these symptoms had to do with the medicine that she was taking for elevated blood pressure, and she was working with her cardiologist to adjust the dosage level to correct her breathing. Some friends of ours arrived for an overnight visit early on June 7. Elsie's classmate and friend from childhood had a very severe cough, which I assumed to be the end of a spring cold. Within a week after our friends left Elsie's breathing seemed to get worse, and she had an extremely bad cough but did not come down with a cold. Several weeks passed, June turned into July, and I kept encouraging her to call her classmate to see what she was taking for her cough, but Elsie wanted to keep her problems to herself.

Our family gathered in Duxbury for a summer vacation in August. Elsie's cough continued, and she became more tired than normal. Her statements were reflecting her fatigue: "This is just too tiring. We really shouldn't suggest a family party again. I need a better bathing facility. Call the plumber and get a quote. What I'd really like is a first-floor separate bedroom and bath, but that will take too long." She began to develop sore muscles and indigestion about four hours after meals.

The children and grandchildren went home, and Elsie attended a routine appointment with her gynecologist at the New England Baptist Hospital on September 17. Although nothing surfaced at that visit, I was becoming increasingly alarmed by her repetitive cough and displays of fatigue, which seemed out of character. She had previously worked uninterrupted from dawn to dusk, but now she was losing focus in her work. I asked her to see a primary-care doctor, but she did not have one; she agreed that she would discuss her symptoms with her cardiologist at her September 23 appointment. Elsie had been using an inhaler, prescribed by her doctor to strengthen her lungs, and she continued to feel that her cough was coming from the medicine. At this point in time, neither of us had even the slightest suspicion of any problem behind the cough. Although there appeared to be no urgency, her cardiologist ordered chest X-rays.

Diagnosis

The X-rays revealed a suspicious area in Elsie's right lung and a follow-up CT scan on October 3 confirmed a large dark area in the right lung. An immediate appointment was scheduled with an oncologist at the New England Baptist Hospital. I am not sure whether or not either of us even knew what an oncologist was, but as we traveled to this appointment, we both began to adjust to the possibility that Elsie might be left with one lung. She was continuing to slow down, complaining about her low energy level, and asking for a nightly back rub to try to relieve an annoying backache.

As we left the house on October 8, Elsie almost blacked out on the way to the car. Just nerves? She met with the oncologist, and I was asked to join the meeting. He reported that the tests to date showed an almost collapsed right lung and a need for some immediate further testing. He scheduled a next-day meeting with a New England Baptist surgeon to discuss symptoms and surgery options. As we drove home, trying to absorb what we had both heard, we talked about the upcoming adjustments we would have to make to our lives. We now knew that whatever the future held, it was a joint venture, and I would be present for almost every appointment and procedure.

There is a certain amount of anxiety preceding any doctor or hospital visit, which is often related to the uncertainties at hand and to the actual time away from home. We were comfortable away from the home phone and leaving two dogs at home, and we started off for the New England Baptist Hospital early in the morning of October 9, planning on being home for lunch. Elsie liked the surgeon, but he told us that a number of tests were needed. She then spent the next five hours undergoing a CT scan, nuclear scan, bronchial scan, chest X-rays, and numerous blood tests. After we had entered thinking we would only be two hours at the hospital, we finally got back into the car by about three in the afternoon. The tests led to a bronchoscopy on October 13, followed by a CT scan of her head, and stress and breathing tests on October 16.

We met with the surgeon again on October 22, at which time he disclosed a diagnosis of lung cancer in Elsie's right lung. He ordered further tests to examine lymph nodes and her back, but told us he would have to withdraw, as the doctor in charge. The tests revealed that cancer had spread beyond her lung, and surgery to remove the lung was not an option. When the surgeon gave her this news, she was very upset. It was no longer a case of losing a lung. She would have to live with an advanced stage of cancer without the emotional support from a surgeon who she admired. This was a big emotional blow to Elsie, who had developed high confidence in the surgeon. As we drove home again, Elsie was fairly explicit: "If for some reason I should not survive, I want you to move as soon as you can to Carleton-Willard Homes." This was a continuing-care retirement community where there were cottages for independent living. She continued, "I also hope that you can find a caring home for our dogs."

The office visit on October 22 was followed by a PET scan and MRI on the next day. With all these tests now completed, we met with the surgeon and the oncologist on October 25. They confirmed lung cancer, spine cancer, and possibly bronchial cancer. They recommended immediate chemo treatments.

On October 27, Elsie and I met again with the oncologist to discuss treatment options. He reported that a realistic life expectancy without treatments was three months, and it would be one to three years with aggressive treatment. This news was not a real shocker, since our anxieties had been on the increase for the whole month. However, neither of us was well informed about cancer, even though many family members had died from cancer. We didn't know anything about treatment options or hospitals specializing in cancer treatment, other than from media reports, but Elsie did have a brother, who had been in charge of a wellness center, who was well informed. We both liked the oncologist, but Elsie was somewhat uncomfortable about continuing with the Baptist where she had had her mastectomy. We both felt that a second opinion was mandatory. Acting on suggestions from the oncologist and others, and an Internet search, we scheduled a meeting with an oncologist at the Dana-Farber Cancer Institute.

The oncologist at the Baptist encouraged one of his cancer survivor patients to call Elsie. She was very outgoing and truthful on the phone and told a real horror story of aggressive treatments, hospitalizations, and near-death experiences, but she was still on her feet and had nothing but praise for her treatment at the Baptist. Long faces and skepticism about the next appointment and possible treatments followed.

Over our long marriage, Elsie and I had successfully worked our way through periods of extreme stress caused by medical problems, business and economic stress, loss of loved ones, and family issues. In the ten years leading up to her diagnosis, we had become closer than in any of the prior years, working together on her poetry and each pursuing special interests and the camaraderie of our growing family. Now, in a period of just four months, all that togetherness came to a sudden halt. Cancer took over our lives and was sending a severe message: "There is no way out." We were overwhelmed, and each of us was trying to understand the enormity of what was coming to pass.

I have an engineering background and have held management positions in both for-profit and not-for-profit organizations. I prided myself on strategic planning skills, the ability to see ahead, establish a plan with checkpoints, identify and solve problems, and successfully conclude a project. I was now thrown into a position with total loss of control, where my talents could not be utilized. There was no way to make day-to-day plans; communication with doctors and caregivers was difficult, since they could not predict the future course of the disease, and I became extremely frustrated.

Second Opinion

Elsie's emotions took the place of fatigue as she prepared for her first appointment at Dana-Farber. Prior to being seen, she had to obtain releases and collect all of the X-rays and CT and MRI scans from the Baptist and other locations and deliver them to Dana-Farber for analysis. Phone calls, frustrating follow-ups, and difficult file searches all stood in the way of a smooth transition.

We arrived on the eleventh floor of Dana-Farber on November 3 and were greeted by a room filled with patients and partners or friends. Appointments were running behind schedule, evoking complaints from both patients and family members. I shared in this discomfort and, looking around the room, observed that there seemed to be three different stages of anxiety. First-timers had that gaunt "what's happening to me?" look, and couples held hands and stayed close in anticipation of unknowns. Repeats came in fashion cap, synthetic wig, or bare head, with a more determined "let's get this over with" face. Coffee, muffins, snacks, soft drinks, water, and fruit were readily available. Weight-challenged patients and family members tanked up on the free offerings, while we stashed fruit for later in the day.

A nurse practitioner finally called Elsie's name, and she went behind doors for a pre-exam physical and blood tests. Eventually, I was invited to join Elsie and the oncologist. He had excellent communication skills, and we were both impressed with his soft-spoken, but honest, presentation. He had reviewed the X-rays and CT and MRI scans and confirmed the diagnosis made at the Baptist. "Based on my observations, you are in stage four, the most advanced stage of lung cancer, and may have had lung cancer for three or four years. The tumors have spread to your spine, but are not yet in your spinal cord. Your prospects are not good: three to six months without treatment, and one to five years with aggressive treatment. You will have to decide within the next week whether or not you want to be treated here or at the Baptist."

This diagnosis was a shocker to both of us. As we drove home, Elsie said she probably did not want to go through chemotherapy. I told her that I would support whatever decision she made, but if it were me, I would opt for the most aggressive treatment, including experimental drugs. Over the next week, she talked to some friends and family members and did not find any support for going without treatment. We had long talks about her future, in which I expressed hope and belief that she would live at least three more years.

We returned to Dana-Farber on November 10. Elsie said that she wanted to be treated there, but she hoped it could be without aggressive treatment. After discussing options, she gave a weak okay to begin treatment. Our expectations were very mixed. Relying on the information from the oncologist, I imagined a course of lifesaving treatment from one of the new experimental drugs. I was now relieved to know that some positive steps were being taken to fight the cancer. Elsie, on the other hand, felt that she was giving in after seriously considering undergoing no treatments at all.

Beginning Treatment

Once Elsie had agreed to treatment, her oncologist wasted no time and initiated treatment on November 10. He presented a program that sounded too good to be true. Elsie was over seventy and had not had chemotherapy treatments. Therefore, she was qualified for a trial program that was proving very effective: a drug called Tarceva was administered once a day by a pill taken at home. This procedure eliminated the weekly trips to Dana-Farber for the more traditional infusion treatments. However, she still needed to visit once a month for blood tests, steroids, and Zometa, a bone-strengthening medication. These were administered by infusion, on the tenth floor of the Dana-Farber building, where there were patients receiving chemotherapy for a wide variety of cancer conditions.

Our first visit to the tenth floor on the afternoon of November 10 turned out to be a "wait-and-see" game. There was a big noontime backup of patients, ranging in age from the twenties to the eighties, waiting for treatment. We had arrived thinking in terms of an hour. After several subsequent visits we learned the protocol: blood tests, pharmacy authorizations from the doctor, delivery of the drugs to the tenth floor, verification of patient and drug information, and then infusions. That schedule put us at the exit door about four hours after arrival.

The tenth floor provided more than fifty settings for treatment in private and semiprivate space. Usually two patients received treatment in a curtained-off area, but sometimes there were more, and occasionally we were totally private. Snacks were immediately available, and sandwiches, soft drinks, and yogurt were delivered to a refrigerator serving a section of the floor. I soon learned to monitor deliveries to the refrigerator, picking out the most desirable choices for both patient and partner. Toilet facilities were conveniently located, but Elsie had a fear of being locked in and asked me to stand guard with the door slightly open for each of her many visits.

Four hours provided plenty of time to talk, to eat a snack, or for Elsie just to lie quietly reflecting on what might happen in the future and what had gone on in her life. In view of the lack of privacy, there was more time for reflection than for conversation, and I know that many of Elsie's thoughts returned to her childhood and to our five children.

My own thoughts bounced back and forth between caregiver responsibilities that I had to take on and the frightening prospect that I might lose my partner. Expressing fear in public or private did not seem to fit my character. I tried to smile and converse with other patients, but their very flat responses signaled their own feelings of being locked in a box with no way out.

Life With Tarceva

The early result of using Tarceva was encouraging. The monthly visits for checkups, blood tests, and Zometa, coupled with X-rays and MRIs, showed no further growth of the tumor in Elsie's lung, and her strength and spirits seemed to have stabilized. A mammogram on November 25 confirmed that there was no cancer in her remaining breast.

Life with Tarceva was as good as could be expected, given the knowledge that she now had a finite lifetime—with *finite* being defined as somewhere between one and five years. We had gotten over the shock of her diagnosis and turned our attention to short-term plans. Under her encouragement (I was less than enthusiastic) we made appointments and visited several continuing-care communities. With some reluctance on my part, we made a return visit and left a modest deposit to reserve space for independent housing at Carleton-Willard Homes in Bedford, Massachusetts. Our plan was to move there if her health condition deteriorated or, at the latest, in five or six years—a reasonable match to the Carleton-Willard waiting list for independent living.

We owned homes in Duxbury and Brighton, but neither was suitable for temporary or live-in nursing support. A set of aggressive outside steps led to the first floor of the Brighton house; there was no downstairs bathroom and no legal way to add additional first-floor rooms. Therefore, Elsie carefully scanned every real estate listing, and we spent Sundays and some weekdays looking at possible options in the Boston area—but none in our price range offered a street-level master bedroom and bath and adjoining space for live-in help. Elsie strongly preferred to keep a house in the Boston area with ready access to her doctors, but our search was fruitless.

The monthly visit to Dana-Farber on December 8 was not as encouraging as Elsie's apparent progress. We were told, "We can't really tell for two months if the tumor has been held in check." At this point, I began to spend time on the Internet to learn more about lung cancer and treatment options, and the articles were not very reassuring. Elsie preferred not to read the articles and relied heavily on her intuition and her doctor's counsel about steps forward. We had a family Christmas get-together in Duxbury; there was a cloud overhanging, but she threw herself totally into the party, including a few games of ping-pong.

After the regular monthly visit to Dana-Farber on January 5 for Zometa, we went to a nearby MRI facility on January 7 for a progress check. This turned out to be a devastating experience for Elsie in the enclosed MRI machine. She had always had a problem with being locked in elevators, ski lifts, and other closed spaces like bathrooms, probably the result of being locked in her bedroom as a child. When the test began, with the loud bonging and no apparent communication with the outside world, she began kicking and screaming, "Let me out!" The technician finally (it could have been immediately) responded, and Elsie left the facility in tears. Subsequent arrangements were made to use an open MRI at the Brigham and Women's Hospital, where an understanding technician talked her through the exam. The results were a mixed bag. There was no increase in the lung tumor, but it looked like cancer was beginning to spread to other parts of her body.

The visits to Dana-Farber on February 2 and 23 provided no new information, but our spirits were fairly high, since Tarceva seemed so easy. Her sore back bothered her at night, but she was fairly energetic during the day, and we were living as normal a life as possible under the cloud of cancer. On March 1, she returned to the Brigham and Women's MRI facility, and the report was positive. The tumor seemed to have been held in check, even shrunk a bit. With that news and a follow-up checkup on March 29, we were green-lighted for a trip to Sweden to visit family and Amsterdam to sightsee. "Do whatever you want to do, but try not to overdo," we were told.

Unknown Time Lines

Considering the plane flights and all the ground that we covered in our trip overseas, I felt that Elsie was in pretty good shape. In fact, after a tiring week in Sweden with family, she appeared to have more stamina for walking around and sightseeing in Amsterdam than I did. We visited important points of interest such as Dam Square, the Van Gogh Museum, and the Anne Frank house. I could not help silently drawing a parallel between Anne Frank being locked in her house and Elsie locked in her body with cancer. I have no idea whether or not such thoughts were in her mind.

We returned from our trip in good spirits, and the April 26 visit to Dana-Farber resulted in another okay. However, though words were unspoken, we both knew that bad news might be coming—but we were both thinking in terms of years, not months. We began to change our lifestyle, with many more meals out, going to movies, and visiting local friends we hadn't seen in years.

We continued to look for new housing in the Brighton area, but found no keepers. Maybe we should add a master bedroom and bath to the Duxbury house where we have room to add on, we thought. Housing concerns remained front and center in our minds, but any thoughts of clearing up personal affairs before an uncertain end-of-life date were dismissed in favor of things that could be accomplished in the near term. Elsie claimed, "No, I don't really want to talk about what to do with my poetry (there were ten thousand poems to be vetted!) or my paintings. Maybe when I go, you should just truck all of the poems off to the dump—but I always did want to publish at least one more of my manuscripts, with an attractive multicolored outer cover. Maybe one of the children could help."

As her spouse, I was totally sympathetic to her ongoing discomfort, but very unsettled by the unknown time lines. In addition to the poetry, there were hundreds of her oil paintings and pastels, as well as an art collection and personal items that needed to have children's names put on them. I needed some guidance and felt that there was a sneaker wave on the way that was going to bring havoc to our lives. I pleaded, "How can we keep talking about a move, with time getting short?" "Don't worry; I know there must be a house out there for us, and you ought to be able to find it. We have plenty of time to make a move," she would say.

The sneaker wave arrived on May 3. Blood tests and X-rays returned the unsettling news that Tarceva had lost its punch. "Cancer cells have spread. You have only a few months to live without switching to a new medication, or six months or more with chemo: Carboplatin and Paclitaxel (Taxol)." "What happens if they don't work?"

"We have ten or more different drugs in trial stages. If one doesn't work, we can try another. Not untypically, cancers can be controlled for six months or so, but then they reinvent themselves in a form resistant to the current drug regime."

We had a difficult time digesting this new information and were beginning for the first time to understand that there are holding actions, and that for fourth-stage lung cancer there might be miracles, but there are no reliable cures. Therefore, any program selected became a further step into unknown territory, possibly accompanied by loss of mobility and dignity. Elsie's initial reluctance to undergo aggressive chemo treatment was still there, but, after further discussion with her doctor, she decided to start a new program.

Taxol and Carboplatin

The new protocol started in May, with infusions on May 3, 10, and 17. This new series resulted in a real knockdown in round one, when both Taxol and Carboplatin were infused, followed by two weeks of just Taxol, and then two weeks off for Elsie's system to recover before the next round. She came home to bed after round one, which typically was on a Monday, with some energy the next day, but not full recovery until Friday or Saturday. She was opposed to taking any painkillers except for Tylenol and Benadryl and was very sore, unable to find a comfortable position in bed. The nightly back rub became a "must have" rather than a soothing ease into sleep.

The side effects began to show themselves almost immediately, as her hair began to fall out. We both visited the ninth floor of Dana-Farber on May 25 to look over alternative headpieces, such as caps and wigs. Fortunately, we found a wig that was a very good match with her hair color and style. On her next infusion visit, I picked out five caps, which turned out to be her constant companions until her final hospitalization. Within a month, she had lost all of her hair, embarrassing her to the point that she did not want to be seen in my presence unless fully covered. The mastectomy in 2002 had been an indignity. The complete loss of hair took someone who placed a high value on her appearance to a new low.

For the first round of monthly infusions we arrived on the eleventh floor of Dana-Farber at nine in the morning for her physical exam and blood workup. If blood test results were within appropriate limits (there was only one time when they were not), we moved to the tenth floor to wait for space for multiple infusions, which took about four hours. Elsie received Zometa for bone treatment, painkiller, and Taxol and Carboplatin, all intravenously. These hospital visits typically took up most of the day. We left home about eight fifteen in the morning and arrived back to two anxious dogs by late afternoon.

Infusions on June 1 and 7 continued to sap Elsie's strength, but we both wanted to attend our granddaughter's graduation from the University of Oregon, in Eugene, Oregon. Although we had made this trip several times in the past, Elsie was very apprehensive. "I'll wear a wig for the graduation ceremonies, but what if it falls off? How about using the bathrooms on the plane and in the airport? Will you stand by? I think I can do it, but I don't want to faint and I'm not sure whether or not I'll have enough energy to carry this off." Nevertheless, we made the trip without any serious mishaps and returned to Dana-Farber on June 15 for round three of that month's treatments.

In the treatment area, one next-bed patient appeared to be a media reporter finishing and editing her latest story online on her laptop. Another person in that day's cubicle of four talked boastfully about winning a two year battle with prostate cancer and "still doing it." Patient number four had fallen asleep holding a cup of some beverage, which was starting to spill over into his lap. Should I have interfered or called the already-too-busy floor nurse? Across the aisle, an attractive mid-thirties couple stayed close together, hand in hand, while he was infused. I tried to keep up a good front, running errands for snacks and sandwiches, but after three hours I had seen enough of the Boston skyline. Elsie looked out the window with a blank stare that suggested that she was reaching back in time for happier days. I felt the pain of the procession of patients, and I itched to be on my way with a slightly unsteady partner hanging on to my left arm. All the time I was trying to adjust to the message that any treatment protocol was trial and error and could be short-lived. There were going to be some good days, but this was not one of them. I needed to get out of there before I became one of them.

We left home on June 28 after lunch and arrived back after eight in the evening. This was probably our longest and most frustrating visit to the tenth and eleventh floors of Dana-Farber. Nothing special—just delay after delay after delay. One cannot spend that much time at Dana-Farber without absorbing some of the strain and fear of patients who are wheeled by on gurneys or in wheelchairs. There is no joking around, no shining faces, and nothing to relieve the tension. Cancer has nearly every patient in its grip, and both patients and caretakers just go through the motions. As a partner, I tried being positive, but deep down I felt that I was failing. Elsie was silently calling for me to help, but I was powerless to respond.

Keeping Up a Good Front

A patient participates in a treatment program with hope that the treatments will slow down or halt the spread of cancer. Without that hope, there would be no point in trying a new regimen. We continued our weekly visits to Dana-Farber with increased apprehension about the impact of the new chemo program. The July 12 visit began with an X-ray at Brigham and Women's, and Elsie's oncologist reported, "Good news! The tumor is shrinking. We'll take a confirming MRI and schedule the next series beginning July 19." Our spirits were lifted by this report, but the pictures presented by the X-ray and MRI didn't seem to square with Elsie's condition.

Elsie had begun to tire more easily, but was still determined to show a good face. She did not have any nausea or other side effects, but she now slept from soon after supper until after six thirty in the morning, compared with her former schedule of after ten thirty in the evening until sunrise. She began to experience some dizziness, particularly when she first stepped out of the car, but with the frequency increasing to several times a day. She attributed this to a buildup of the toxins in her body and, for the first time, began talking about quality of life and the possibility of discontinuing treatment. In retrospect, she had probably entered a phase of "let's get this over with," while I still hoped for and expected an extended period of recovery.

We often went to our favorite Chinese restaurant at the Chestnut Hill mall. She was very pleased to be recognized by the maitre d' who seated us in a quiet area behind a back partition. I suspect that we were always seated there to shield new customers from the view of a green-, blue-, or yellow-capped cancer patient as they entered, but that thought never occurred to her. We attended a fiftieth wedding anniversary, where a close friend said she loved Elsie's new hairdo. I had to confide that it was synthetic and embarrass our friend. The wig was worn on only a few occasions, but it did look natural and becoming. At Kmart, she received an unsolicited compliment from a sales assistant: "You are really beautiful" (in that blue cap). She didn't mind being in the public eye with a cap, but she wanted me nearby while she shopped, due to dizziness. Nevertheless, she still walked alone at the Duxbury beach or around Chandler Pond in Brighton. She stopped driving by herself by the end of July.

Children and family were kept informed by phone calls with Elsie, and in July neither she nor I revealed details of her decline. In the past, we had traditionally hosted a family gathering on Cape Cod and encouraged the children and grandchildren to come to Duxbury in August. They would then have a chance to have some face-to-face discussions and also get some time at the beach. The family had use of the Duxbury house while we commuted from Brighton. This plan allowed time and space for Elsie and me to get away from the fray and let Elsie rest.

Terminating Chemotherapy

The third in a series of infusions for chemotherapy was on August 2, followed by two weeks off, when the family came to Duxbury for the vacation. Elsie was beginning to have more dizzy periods, particularly when she first stood up, but insisted on continuing her daily walk on the beach. I am sure that the combination of sea air and time to be alone with her thoughts was a happy diversion from the regular trips to Dana-Farber.

As the month progressed, she needed to have me nearby to correct her balance, to keep her from bumping into a wall, or to keep her from falling. We continued to split our time between Duxbury and Brighton, although Duxbury was becoming an unwelcome commute as the frequency of pit stops increased. After the next series of infusions on August 16, 23, and 30, her doctor recommended that the treatments be stopped to try to find out what was causing the dizziness. He must have seen these signs in other patients before, but he did not leap to conclusions. The word *fear* didn't even begin to express our emotions, and our anxieties rose to new levels as we waited for the results of the next MRI.

An early morning MRI at the Brigham and Women's Hospital on September 2 revealed that the Taxol and Carboplatin treatments had shrunk the lung tumor and checked the spread of cancer in her bones. However, we were told that the chemo treatment had probably not stopped the spread of cancer to her brain. Her doctor explained that MRIs are helpful but probably not of sufficient resolution to identify small tumors in the brain, which could very well be causing Elsie's dizziness. He recommended ten sequential days of radiation in addition to the chemotherapy. I had watched the wife of a business partner go through the same treatment before she died and was not unhappy when Elsie said, "No way." Another option was to see a neuro-oncology specialist. Elsie asked for the latter and was referred to one at Dana-Farber/Brigham and Women's Cancer Center. His first available appointment was in two weeks.

Elsie continued to have dizzy spells and balance problems. On the night of September 8 she almost fainted, falling into her bureau on the way to the bathroom, skinning her arm and leg in a bloody mess. In the morning, I insisted that she contact her oncologist to see if he could ask the neuro-oncologist to move her appointment up. She was seen the same day and the neuro-oncologist recommended an MRI of the entire spine and possibly a spinal tap, depending on the results.

We returned to the house after an admittedly tiring visit, and, as we were walking up the steps with Elsie firmly holding onto my arm, without warning, she completely collapsed. Unforeseen and alarming as it was, her collapse left me helpless to hold her limp body up, and she fell onto the cement walk, skinning her knee. Afterwards she had no recollection of passing out. I spent the day in a state of shock. She spent the rest of the day in bed.

Rough Water

Early in the morning on September 10, Elsie called for my assistance on her way back to bed from the bathroom. As I tried to help her, she completely collapsed and fainted face-down on her knees with her head buried in the mattress. I yelled and yelled her name, but there was no response for what appeared to be several minutes, but was probably thirty to sixty seconds.

Immediate phone calls to the neuro-oncologist were not returned until ten thirty in the morning. He recommended that she report to the Brigham and Women's emergency room for evaluation. Even though Elsie had had nearly a year of contact with Dana-Farber and Brigham and Women's, she had to line up in the emergency area with all of the other patients of the day and wait her turn: to the right a broken finger, across the hall an apparently homeless youth with limited attire and unknown problems, a bandaged and bruised face to the left, and lots of activity behind closed doors from patients being brought in by ambulance. Preliminary findings were inconclusive, and she collapsed to the floor while being taken down for an X-ray. Six hours after our arrival, she was finally admitted for evaluation. I returned home in despair, questioning what appeared to be the slow wheels of justice for my bride of fifty-two years.

Elsie was taken down for a CT scan, but again she collapsed while trying to get onto the exam table and had to be lifted from the floor by four attendants. Collapses were not yet directly linked to seizures, but that's what was triggering her falls. On Saturday, September 11, she was told to defer eating and drinking in anticipation of an MRI, but emergencies tied up the MRI equipment all day. An early morning MRI scan was promised for Sunday. With prior patient experience and good sense, one of the nurses asked if Elsie had an up-to-date Health Care Proxy. She did not and immediately executed one, which turned out to be a critical step in her end-of-life treatment.

She had another poor night, during which she collapsed to the floor and was found frothing at the mouth. She was very apprehensive about the MRI and said she probably could not go through the exam without an attendant anesthesiologist. "You'll have to wait until Monday," is what she was told. After a reasonably good night on Sunday, with no apparent seizures, Elsie then waited all day Monday, again without liquids or meals, for the MRI. It never happened. There were no strings to pull, she was increasingly uncomfortable, and as a "team" we were beginning to feel like abandoned sheep.

Who's In Charge?

There seemed to be a change in responsibility for Elsie's care that occurred after her admission to Brigham and Women's via the emergency room. Although her oncologist at Dana-Farber was still in the background offering diagnosis opinions, the neuro-oncologist had dropped out of the picture, and day-to-day responsibility had been handed over to the Brigham and Women's ER admitting doctor. When we first met him, he looked like an ER doctor from a TV drama. Elsie shared my apprehension about being handed from doctor to doctor, and, as her condition continued to deteriorate, she began to plead to go home. As result of the awkward weekend timing of the MRIs that never happened, she had had little to eat or drink after admission, and she lost interest in eating. Her oncologist promised to get over (cross the bridge connecting Dana-Farber to Brigham and Women's) and to send a Dana-Farber palliative care team, but he confirmed that the Brigham and Women's doctor was now in charge.

Maybe I should have been more demanding and asked for a private meeting with the Brigham and Women's doctor, to develop some sense of what was immediately ahead, but he seemed to be totally stressed out. I did not ask for such a meeting. I was trying to keep some sanity in my own life, with four or five visits each day to the hospital alternating with time at home for the dogs and other responsibilities. I had an enormous feeling of guilt and was frustrated that I could not do more. I did not understand the relationship between Dana-Farber and Brigham and Women's and did not feel that the best available doctor was watching over Elsie's care. In fact, we were not given an opportunity to choose. By nature and training, I am a control freak and am most comfortable with a plan, a series of alternatives, and checkpoints to see if progress is being achieved. At this point, there was no plan, and I didn't know what to expect or how to measure progress. I suspect that Elsie knew that only she was in charge of her destiny.

For the next four or five days seizures increased, and her breathing deteriorated. She would partially raise her arm as if to point to the sky, then go into a blank stare, and then faint. She had no recollection of these events and occasional checks by nurses turned into round-the-clock observation. New medicines were prescribed to try to reduce the number of seizures, and painkillers were added for headaches that followed the seizures. The nurses were very helpful but needed occasional encouragement. I took on the role of part-time nurse after they showed me where to get cold packs and other necessities.

In her more lucid moments, Elsie continued to ask to go home. However, the doctors felt that cancer had moved to her upper spine and that she should not leave the hospital until a complete diagnosis had been made. Their message quieted her somewhat, but she was still not calm. Since she tired so quickly, and since I still held out the view that she had several months or longer to live, I put off visitors, including family. She accepted incoming phone calls, but I tried to limit those, as they seemed to tire her out and would be followed by more seizures. I felt very two-faced: acting as the gatekeeper, hoping that rest would cure the seizures, but knowing that our children, as well as her siblings, wanted to meet her face to face to offer prayers and support.

Meeting of Minds?

A week after Elsie's admission to Brigham and Women's there was a confluence of pressures coming from the doctors, the family, and from Elsie. She had been put on oxygen, in an attempt to improve her breathing. The predicted worst-case scenario was that she might not recover from a seizure. A spinal tap showed that small tumors had moved into the upper spine and had probably reached the brain. Her doctors were trying to stabilize her condition to prepare her for release from the hospital and hinted to me that that could be in another few days. I had not even thought in those terms, believing that she would remain in the hospital and would be relocated to a nursing home only if a significant lifetime extension was forecast.

I had been holding back family visits, but began to receive impassioned calls for permission to visit from our children, who were rightfully concerned. When one of our sons and his wife arrived, Elsie had a reasonably good day, but repeated her plea to return home or move to a hospice house. We had no experience with hospice. I don't know where Elsie had heard about hospice houses, but my son, his wife, and I began to look at alternative end-of-life facilities. Our first visit to Tippett House was very upsetting. By pure happenstance, my brother-in-law's step-daughter was in one of the rooms that we were shown and she was taking her last breaths before she died the next day.

I thought that the Nursing Center at Carleton-Willard Homes might be a possibility, since we were now on the waiting list for housing. What I heard was: "Sorry, no room at this time. Our first priority is given to residents. Maybe a room will free up in a week or so." When another son arrived a week later, we looked at Sherrill House, Goddard, and Wingate, in Brighton, but none of these seemed to measure up to Carleton-Willard. The family search for a nursing center or hospice house was not helped at all when a young intern checked in on Elsie one day and told her that she could be discharged to go home any time she wanted to, even that afternoon. I had to counter with a promise to continue to keep looking. "You really haven't done a thorough job. If I were looking, I am sure I could find a better place than Carleton-Willard in the greater Boston area, or, somehow, we could work it out at home."

At this juncture there seemed to be no solution and no meeting of minds. Elsie wanted to go home, the doctors wanted to discharge a patient whose status could not be improved, and there was no readily acceptable alternative living space available with round-the-clock support.

Tight Quarters

Elsie's last ten days at Brigham and Women's were filled with multiple seizures, which produced extreme fatigue. Her doctors tried different combinations of drugs to try to slow down the rate of seizures, some of which were successful; others produced disturbing side effects, like the lowering of her sodium level to dangerous levels. She received Dilantin to replace Tegretol for controlling the seizures and for a few days was down to one nighttime seizure. Nevertheless, the rails were raised on her bed, and she was being monitored around the clock to make sure that she did not try and get out of bed, as she had done, resulting in a fall and surface injuries. The nurse's message to me while I was there was quite clear: "Please tell us when you leave the room. We don't want another fall."

In order to help her rest and return the sodium levels to acceptable limits, Klonopin was added to the drug list. Elsie had always been not more than an hour or two away from a glass of water, but was told that she had to keep fluid intakes to a minimum to prevent flushing the sodium out of her system. At one point, her doctor said that he was not sure whether or not a major seizure that had just occurred was the result of cancer or the medication. This was both disturbing (Why don't they know?) and encouraging to me, leading me to believe that if the correct balance of drugs could be achieved, her condition would stabilize and not deteriorate. However, to Elsie the message was devastating. She basically stopped taking any liquids or food and talked with difficulty about final arrangements. She favored some sort of religious service, ideally in Trinity Church in Boston, where we had attended services for many years. She wanted to publish at least one more book but was not sure what to do with the rest of the poems. She felt that the kids could divide up the artwork.

In spite of all the complications, Elsie still felt driven to write poetry. She asked for a dictating machine, but she was beginning to lose her sight and could not see well enough to punch the keypad. I punched the right buttons while she dictated her last poem, "A Personal View," about the caregivers at Brigham and Women's.

The children were now making regular visits, leaving me feeling somewhat exasperated, since she confided to me that each visit really tired her out. She might have one good night, but then she would have nights with many seizures and little rest at all. She increased her pleas to get out of the hospital and go home, where she thought she would be better off, not ever accepting my response that it would be impossible to do so. In spite of confirmation from the children that the Carleton-Willard Nursing Center was the best prospect to pursue, she felt that she was being maneuvered for my comfort and not hers. We had discussed end-of-life housing in depth during the summer and had concluded that there was no way she could be a patient in our Brighton house. Now we were faced with returning to two dogs (which she loved) in the house, no first-floor bathroom, difficult logistics to get her up the steps into the house, given her condition—not to speak of my role finding round-the-clock, at-home nursing care, chasing doctors to get approval for continuing or new medications, providing food and necessities, and answering an increased number of phone calls from our extended families.

My daily phone calls to Carleton-Willard turned from inquiries to pleas for help. By this time the doctors had made it clear to me that there was not much more that they could do. "We'll have to discharge her in a few days." I pleaded with them to give me a few more days to see where Elsie might go, and they promised to work with me, but they said that Tuesday, September 28 was the outside date. The nurse coordinator at Brigham and Women's was working hard to find an acceptable solution. At the same time, on September 25, Elsie almost had a seizure while I was helping her put on her sweater, but she asked for and consumed some soup and cake at lunchtime. "I'm ready to go home now," she said.

Finally, a break came, on the weekend. The nurse coordinator contacted the person who was responsible for Nursing Center admissions and a room became available at Carleton-Willard. Elsie was transferred at noontime on September 27, with a new problem: an infection caused by a catheter. She encountered many seizures en route, and she was given a nice private room with a tree-line view.

The hospital discharge certificate listed eighteen medications: Tylenol, Atenolol (blood pressure), Klonopin (seizures), Decadron (steroid), Benadryl (antihistamine), Colace (stool softener), Ibuprofen (headache), Ativan (anxiety), Milk of Magnesia, Reglan (nausea), Dilantin (seizures), Sarna (itching), Demeclocycline (sodium), Lovenox (blood clots), K-Dur (potassium), Maalox (upset stomach), Levoflaxacin (antibiotic), and Bacitracin (antibiotic).

Final Weeks

The bright and sunny room at Carleton-Willard's Nursing Center gave me positive energy and a great sense of relief that Elsie would receive excellent care for her final days. However, I was in denial and still thinking in terms of months, not weeks. I just could not accept the truth that the end was in sight and did not feel that a round-the-clock vigil by the children was appropriate.

Fortunately, they were more sensitive to the reality of Elsie's condition and soon set up regular extended visits, while I tried to keep things together both at Carleton-Willard and at home. There were contracts to understand and sign, a mortician to be selected, doctors at Dana-Farber and Brigham and Women's to be checked with, and an extended family to be constantly updated. At this point her siblings arrived, and there was almost no time that a family member was not present.

The sunny room was not at all welcoming to Elsie. Her sight was going; she could not stand bright light, and she asked to have the blinds drawn. She was not allowed out of bed but tried to get to the bathroom at night when no one was around, fell, and skinned her knee. The Nursing Center was quite a change from the hospital where she had been under a twenty-four-hour watch and a doctor was within easy reach. Here, there were frequent checks by a floor nurse at night, but no full-time monitoring. Her bodily functions began to fail, with almost total loss of bladder control. On the other hand, she asked for some soup one day, almost the first nourishment in a week, and wanted to sign some end-of-life donation checks. I prepared some for her signature and guided her hand, but she could not see what she was signing. The nursing care was excellent, but the nurses could not keep the bed dry, and I had to pinch-hit. I bought additional nightgowns and took three or four home each night to thoroughly cleanse.

Soon after her arrival we needed to execute "no transfer" documents to confirm to Carleton-Willard that Elsie did not want to return to the hospital for a life-ending hookup to monitors and tubes. However, she was still holding out hope for home and did not want to sign papers that she felt locked her into Carleton-Willard. After clarification from Carleton-Willard administration, the children and I learned that she could always be signed out to go home even though "no transfer" documents had been executed. I went ahead, as authorized agent under the Health Care Proxy that she had executed at the hospital, and signed the documents.

Elsie's seizures continued, and she tired easily under increasingly heavy medication. One son began a daily foot massage, which seemed to improve her mood. About a week after her arrival she completely lost her depth perception and needed assistance holding a cup. She continued to lobby in favor of a return to Brighton. She told me that I could learn the necessary therapy to take over full-time care of her at home, and her pleading became increasingly demanding: "I am lonely here; I don't want to stay here; I want to come home. The nurses are slow to answer my calls at night. If you won't let me come home, I could stay with my sister. You haven't tried hard enough to find a better place than this. You are selfish and not willing to help. I'm going to get out of bed and leave here on my own." All of these frantic appeals really stung me, especially when played against my terrifying experience of one month ago, when my lifelong partner had dropped at my feet without any prior warning. Only after meeting with a hospice professional in subsequent days did I learn that such statements were not unusual for a person whose bodily functions had shut down and whose end of life was approaching.

One of our sons could read the signs better than I could and kept urging me to get hospice involved. I finally relented and contacted an office suggested by Dana-Farber. On October 7, two of my children and I had a very rewarding meeting with a Bereavement Coordinator from Health Care Dimensions Hospice. We had a long list of questions after her presentation and she had answers for every one. We learned that a hospice team would not replace Carleton-Willard professional caregivers, but would act as consultants providing help and suggestions for Elsie's care. Those suggestions could be very specific, such as changes in drugs to relieve pain, or more general, such as helping family members understand the psychological and spiritual needs as Elsie approached the end of her life. We immediately felt that hospice organizations had a depth of knowledge in end-of-life matters that we and Carleton-Willard did not have. As impressed as I was, I was fixed in my mind on at least weeks, not days, and said I would call her back. In retrospect, that was a "hiding behind the truth" response to the urgency at hand. The children could see what I could not, and I refused to pick up the signals or believe my eyes.

The visual signals were painful, and I had to live with the guilt and frustration of not being able to stop the clock to keep time from taking away my partner and closest friend. For so many years we had found the inner resources to help each other resolve difficult issues in which emotions boiled to the surface. Now emotions were running out of control for both of us, and there was no time left to peacefully conclude our long relationship.

Troubling Times

The hospice representative said that she would like to see Elsie. As we walked back toward her room, we saw her being wheeled down the hall by a physical therapist who somehow had been able to get Elsie out of bed. This was the first time she had moved from the room since arrival. I took over pushing the gurney out onto a balcony and into some sun, but she shielded her eyes, tired quickly after fifteen minutes in the fresh air, and wanted to return to her room.

She slept for about two hours, and when she woke up she was very uncomfortable and took a while to get settled. I told her what we had learned from the hospice coordinator and asked her about end-of-life directives. This was a mistake on my part and triggered an *I'm locked in!* expression of fear and annoyance, which led to a very heated exchange between us. I think that since she had made it onto the gurney, she jumped to the conclusion that there would be no difficulty traveling home. "This is cruel and unusual punishment!" she cried. Pleas of "I want to come home" were repeated, now in desperate tones. Elsie was very strong-willed and still had fight left in her, but all signs indicated a steady decline. Prior thoughts of frustration flashed through my mind: How could I find three shifts of nurses? Would they allow the dogs in the house while they were there? What about changing and getting new medicines? With what I had been through already, I knew that I wouldn't rest for one minute if she came home, and in the end that would have broken both of us. I relayed that message, but her mind was set.

That night, Elsie tried to get out of bed to go to the bathroom and collapsed, incurring additional abrasions. When she got up off the floor on her own, she couldn't seem to contact the floor nurse and tried to call me. Unfortunately, she could not remember our first-floor Brighton number (we had two separate lines) and her call ended up on the message machine line in our cellar. I happened to be on the other line in the kitchen, talking to my brother-in-law, when she called and never heard the "Please come immediately" message until I checked overnight messages in the cellar the next morning.

I rushed to Carleton-Willard as soon as I heard her message, but did not arrive until about nine thirty in the morning. We had another heated conversation in which she was wild-eyed as she moved in and out of communication. The conversation ended with: "You're the most selfish person I have ever known." In retrospect, I think that this statement was a reversion to the exact language that her mother had used when they crossed wires over a real estate transaction and ended up on nonspeaking terms for almost a year. Of course, her statement was the ultimate sting to me. I was exhausted, did not take it lightly, and felt helpless to provide any comforting thoughts. "What can I do? Is this the way that her life will end?"

At this point, family members began a long vigil. Elsie was given increased doses of medicine to calm her down, but there were lots of agitated hand movements, seizures, and expressions of discomfort. She stopped taking any sips of water and began to pull at the bed sheets and her bedclothes. She became noncommunicative, her sight was gone, and there was no further conversation. The nursing staff was providing outstanding care, but except for changing the bed, there wasn't much more that they could do. The children continued to press for hospice. I continued in denial, but finally agreed to place another call to hospice.

A Kiss Good-bye

I called the hospice facility early on Sunday morning, October 10, only to learn that staff was not in on Sunday but would be available on Monday. My follow-up call early Monday morning produced an automated response: "This is Columbus Day and no staff are on duty." I left urgent messages and finally received a call back from the nurse on duty for the holiday, but she left the main switchboard number for my callback and that number produced the same recorded holiday greeting. After several additional panic calls to every number I could think of, I reached the on-call holiday nurse. She agreed to come to Carleton-Willard at two in the afternoon to meet with the children and me.

Elsie had apparently gotten up during the night, with assistance, to use the bathroom, and she was sipping some ginger ale, about the only liquid she had consumed in several days. This seemed to confirm my judgment that she still had a week or more to live. She was fairly heavily sedated, but asked more than once, "What time is it?" Who knows what was going on in her mind?

The hospice nurse immediately took over and provided much-needed emotional support for all of us. She recommended some medication changes for Elsie to help ease her suffering, and then she left around four thirty. The children continued an all-night vigil. The recommended new medication arrived around eight thirty in the evening, but did little to correct a new pattern of irregular breathing: big breath, then long pause before short gasps. By midnight this had changed to a cough-like breathing. The children wanted to spend the night with Elsie. I was exhausted and returned to Brighton around midnight to get some sleep.

Our oldest daughter called me at two fifteen in the morning on October 12 to say that Elsie's breathing had deteriorated. The nurses wanted to hook her up to oxygen, but that seemed to be in conflict with Elsie's end-of-life wishes. As I rushed to get dressed to return to Carleton-Willard, my daughter called again to say that "Mom has taken her last breath." The next few hours were ones of shock and disbelief, as each of us spent some private time saying our good-byes. I leaned down and kissed her warm lips, still in disbelief that my lifelong partner had left this world. After a six-hour break back at home to get some rest, I returned and leaned down to give Elsie one last kiss. I was startled: her lips were cold, and confusion turned to grief. A numbness took over that did not fade away for weeks, while I grappled with the knowledge that she had left this life, but that we would be together, always.

Preface

Following Elsie's mother's death in February 2003 Elsie and her siblings sorted through hundreds of pictures, letters, and postcards to select memorabilia. This experience prompted Elsie to add to her poems previously written about her family. Several of these poems are included in *Moving on into Morning*. She also began to write down early childhood experiences that might someday be included in an autobiography. The paragraphs that follow were written in April 2003, several months before the first signs of her terminal illness surfaced. These remembrances from her first six years are in first-draft form, but they provide important clues to who Elsie was and who she wanted to be.

Early Years

My mother recently died and I've been sorting through old photographs of the past. My life is more than just myself. Now, as I near seventy years of age, I can look back at an era of amazing change, a history the same, and yet vastly different from, that of any other family member, friend, or culture. I'm but a particle, a stitch in the torn fabric of an at-present split ozone.

I was born to breath on May 29, 1933. My mother got ptomaine poisoning after eating chicken salad at the Devon Horse Show, and that started her labor. It must have been awful, but of course I can't recall. I was bottle-fed by a nurse and probably spoiled rotten as a toddler. My first memory is of walking in a pair of new white shoes. I'm told my first two words were "see man." Soon I pointed up through waving green trees at a propeller plane and said "see leab." If I do say so, I was cute: "by self" girl, golden curls and all.

There was a little girl
and she had a little curl

in the middle of her forehead.
And when she was nice
she was very, very nice;
but when she was not
she was horrid.

My brother, Joe, was born seventeen months later. I pushed him around into the bushes, but secretly I loved his company. My mother's face was white as early sky with freckles: tarnished stars. My father's face wore a full moon's shape. I adored him from the very start of memory. I had to wear an iron brace to straighten out a curving foot, and I tossed and turned and sometimes cried *bloody murder* like my brother.

My third year came with a grand birthday surprise, a Mae West kit: fruity makeup, hat, and faux fur stole. I would laugh and sway the way she did and say, "Come up and see me sometime." I was no Shirley Temple, but I sure could steal the show that way during cocktail hour before the grownups had their dinner.

At age four things began to blur. My mother's swelling tummy sent her to the hospital again. After ten days she came home thin, but with no baby. I didn't know he was stillborn. All I knew was that my mother had changed. She got cross with my father and brother, Joe, but I was given a piebald pony to ride. We entered lead-line classes and won a lot of colored ribbons. In the stable, Charlie Grove braided the pony's mane and tail with red or blue wool.

The next sibling was a sister, five years younger than me. I was growing chubby. Nothing seemed to fill my hunger, not even ice cream cones. Every winter we went to Coconut Grove, Florida, for three months. Daddy had a pet monkey, and Mummy had a red dachshund named Matea. Joe and I went together to preschool there. We learned to swim a little by hanging on to a pole and then letting go. Dear Woo, Miss Wolf, the nurse—who was fat and didn't know how to swim—once did the splits when she put one foot in the boat and left the other on the dock, because she was afraid to jump. She landed in the icy canal with her skirt swishing up like a mushroom above her head. This caused even Mummy to laugh, but it must have been awful for poor Woo. Daddy threw her a life ring and drew her to shore. Dear Woo. Where are you now?

When I was six I had to have my throat painted with gentian violet, and then finally my tonsils got yanked. Back home, I wouldn't stay in bed, though I was meant to rest. Once, Miss Cary—a registered nurse, starched and stiff and totally unsuitable to care for children—locked me in my bedroom. I crayoned every square of my bed pad a color of the rainbow. Miss Cary slapped me hard, and I hemorrhaged from the holes in my throat. Back in the hospital, I kicked and screamed and gagged and blanked out—and then caught an infectious disease. I almost died, I'm told, until an experimental sulfa drug saved me. Say *Ah*! Say *Oh*! But, oh, how I hated that white-coated doctor who swabbed my throat and depressed my tongue with Popsicle sticks till I gagged.

James I. Stockwell

First Memory of Me

My name is Elsie
wea, pointing at
a seaplane:
  a leaf:
  a bird:
in the blue;
  see man,
  see "leab,"
  see moon,
  see sea,
still murmuring
  "by self do"
while wetting
  the first
pair of new
white shoes.

Elsie Wear Stockwell

What Lasts?

My mother's mother
died of breast cancer
before I was born.
I never saw her
except as painted
by Mary Cassatt.
Framed by gilt,
that recalcitrant, red-haired
little girl sitting back
with high-buttoned shoes
in a French blue
velvet armchair,
always presided
above the fireplace
in my parents' living room.

Daddy's mother died
when I was two.
I am told she was very beautiful
and an intellectual.
I only remember
that she smelled good
and felt warm.
Then suddenly her form
wasn't there anymore.
Where did she go?
On a guest room wall
there's a sweet oval
oil of her as a young girl
done by some unknown
amateur.

Plunket

Mummy's snub-nosed father,
pink-faced from galloping a horse
in Unionville, rode red-coated
with his coupled pack
of English foxhounds
through tall copses
and long green valleys
between rounded hills.
After cub hunting he'd ask
everyone back for a big hunt breakfast
prepared by his staff.
His butler, Leroy, always stood
like a statue behind his chair.

The beautiful mask and brush
of some poor fox
hung in his hall.
I never thought to acknowledge
to myself how awful
this was then because
that was what Mummy did as well.
I was twelve
and adored the excitement
of galloping and soaring
with my beloved dappled horse
through early fall's
cool morning mist.

When Spitfire took the bit
there was no stopping him.
He liked to lead. But I couldn't bear
to see the kill;
and never did.
The sudden silence
of the hounds' voices,
noses to leaf spill,
meant the strong smell of vixen or fox
was lost to copse cover

or had gone to ground
or crossed through river water
and that the kits were safe for now.

Over The Hill

Grandpop

Not an intellectual,
not a lover of books;

but a risk taker
good with stocks
and bonds and family:

a five foot nine, wiry,
strong shoulder to shoulder
team player with a temper
when things went wrong.

Oh, but how I loved
the twinkle in his dark eyes.
What fun he was.

Though he could tear
the cover off a baseball
or carry a pigskin across the goal,

driven by blood within
he hungered to win
at any cost.

He'd lob a ball
over a cripple's head
and make him run.

If he had the right of way
he'd ram a skiff off course
in a little sailboat race.

Always restless, on the go
he dropped dead
relatively young
from a stroke:

James I. Stockwell

the only fight
he couldn't win.

Right of Way!

Daddy's Death Day

Sound of rain, then flames: porch nails.
  Honeysuckle smells.
    Siblings among the hedgerows.
    Was he ready to leave us?
Maybe glad to go?
I remember sweltering.
  His soles felt clammy.
    My hands bled red from gripping
    the end of that metal bed.
Later they blistered.
  How different it is today:
   thick fog, cool and white,
    shimmer-shines like his good ghost
    drawing all the islands close.

My Mother at Eighty-four

She stands with her once
fire-colored hair
like a puff of smoke

and waves to us
from behind the mesh
screen of a blue door.

As we drive up hill
she diminishes
to the size

of a freckle
in my compact's mirror.
Daddy is no longer there.

With that little glass
of pride held before
my streaky face

I can see behind!
This fact never ceases
to amaze me.

I am still a child
as is she
caring for a child.

Little leaks fill our eyes
with everybody's sea
like light years.

This might be
the last time.
Bye-bye.

Spring Glory

Firstborn

Frank breech:
feet first! A daughter
so very different
from me:
dark hair, dark eyes,
a stranger really,
a night owl

almost too full of exuberance!
She wore me out
wanting to play hide and seek
past midnight
when I, truly exhausted
by her siblings,
needed sleep.

She grew rebellious,
went to Dead concerts,
smoked pot and wore her heart
on her T-shirt.
Then I couldn't understand,
but now we agree.

Tough and strong and far
more patient than I am,

she can do what I can't:
intervene, teach, mediate.
This planet's better
because she's with it:
children and animals
in particular.

Second Born

A regular birth:
 head first, free of wonder drugs,
  big, lusty, hungry,
   blond, blue-eyed, a Nordic sort.
    Has always loved a pickup:

sings off key, drives fast.
 Observes, then does things quickly.
  What's that hammering?
   Now he's a developer
    of real estate and sculptor.

An artist at heart,
 too kind for business really,
  will try anything,
   has always had a free style,
    big appetite for living.

Third Born

Always found it hard
to smile: A Gemini
from the start:
two minds, one heart.

An electrician, engineer,
photographer, writer and builder
now with his own simple style.

No matter what
his motto is: measure twice
and cut once. Oh, but beware
of his short fuse.

Make him mad unawares
and he'll piss
on your shoes.

Fourth Born

Another blue-eyed boy.
At nine months he knew
how to get the distant ring
he wanted by sitting still
and pulling its string
towards him.
Student teachers watching oom'd and ah'd.
Even in preschool he kept
rearranging his crayons.
Later he sat on the bench a lot
compared to his brothers
until he went to college
and got recruited for crew.
And yes, his team was number one.
But soon he had no time for rowing.
Instead of sibling rivalry
his own artistic ambition grew.
With increasing discipline
he rid himself of a drinking habit
and nipped arrogance in the bud.
Painting became his passion
and business too.
Now in a distant country
where fields of flowers bloom,
he does what he loves.

Fifth Born, Second Month

I think of her
as a snowdrop:

first flower
of each brand new
New England year:

self silent
now as that little
white bell,
head bent down
as if to question
the ground

from which
each winter hour
rises.

Harbinger of dawn's
vernal equinox,

little bloom of snow
in a patch of light
amid the shrinking shadows
of bare boughs
growing closer to water
where the wings
of gulls and crows
divide the sky
and the clear ocean
abides with dolphins.

You are more
than I know.

Springing for Joy

Chapter 1: Breathing Problems

Summer Solstice Heat

Mid-June it all began.
After every telephoned sentence
I had to stop talking.

All my energy
had flown. I blamed it on
the flower beds:

the sweetest scents
were beautiful tree peonies
and rare roses breathed in.

My friend Alice came to visit.
She had a terrible cough.
I thought I'd caught it,

along with a little nausea.
Something more alien kept
pressing up against my rib

cage and breastbone;
but it wasn't heartburn.
I felt as if I was

three months pregnant:
perhaps a foreign body's
bloodroot grew inside me.

I couldn't stand
the scent of the dogs' coats
or the gas stove's blue rings;

and when in town I stepped
outdoors all I could sense
was trafficy exhaust.

And so I went to the cardiologist.
He thought I had an allergy
and prescribed an inhaler;

but it didn't change
the situation or make me better.
In a month I went again.

Something was definitely wrong,
but routine blood tests
showed nothing strange;

nor was there any oceanic
noise in my chest. Nevertheless
this time he ordered X-rays.

Brighton View

Doctor Dare

This blue paper
gown, you say
I have to wear,
        tears
far too easily
for modesty to bear.

I do not want
to stay here
        so bare naked.
I lost
my innocence years ago.
        Eve fled away;

(who knows where?)
and your office
        is far from Eden.

Doing Something Else

You're right, doctor.
I like to hide behind this plant
that only looks like marijuana
so as not to be so easily observed.

Why should you get to know me
and not I you?
Why can't we be on equal terms?
Why not change the way the system works?

It takes time to adapt.
Nothing's perfect.

You observe me from the front
and then the back,
and then all sides like a lump of clay
you'd like to sculpt and change.

  After taking
  my pulse
  you press
  down and dimple
  my belly button
  like a doorbell.

  Half in love
  and half afraid,
  I tremble like a kid.
  What is this game
  of life
  I still
  don't quite
  know how to play?

James I. Stockwell

Exercising My Lungs

Taking a deep breath in fast
and then letting it all go
            out out out
as long and as far as I can.
            Hush now,
hush, can't you hear at the last
            how stillness sounds
like the sea rattling shells,
pebbles, sea glass and stones
            white white white as
the shore it has found:
fallen stars: rocks worn to sand
            where foam also fell:
granules of ourselves:
meeting points free as gulls
resting on a black buoy without
            a clanging bell.

Rocky Shore

Waiting Room

It's not physical.
  So why does it still hurt?
   I giggle like a
    schoolgirl without a blue book.
    I do this so as not to
cry and embarrass
  myself; tears might gutter up
   quite unstoppably.
    Every fear now surfaces
     impossibly fast at once.
I keep wondering
  why sometimes I can't swallow.
   Why's the doctor late?
    Maybe he's intubating
     somebody. Maybe I'm crazy.

Summer Flowers

Early Fall

First cool day
I lie low on my bed.
Daddy's old navy blanket
covers up my legs.
> Something's wrong with me;
> but I don't know what.
> Whenever I'm sick
> I feel as if I'm being
> punished. It's scary.
I'm not even hungry.
What have I done
to deserve this?
Tomorrow I'm going in
for increasing tests.
> Could it be a foreign body
> like a first trimester
> pregnancy? Or cancer?
> Or West Nile Virus?
Or all the blood pressure
medicines I have to take
in the frail name
of better health?
Or maybe a combination?
> Anyway things can't stay
> the same. Something has to change.
> Today every muscle aches
> to the bone of me.
> I can't even make my own bed.
I can't even lift
a blank canvass to paint.
Old age I say is no accident;
but it sure looks and feels that way.
> Even while I lie still
> on a pullout couch,
> pain's rainbow
hula hoops floor to ceiling round
a reconstructed living room.
I have to wait for my husband

8

to help me up.
I hate to be a burden.
Who was it said:
"He also serves
who only stands and waits."?

Day's end

10

Chapter 2: Diagnosis

I Drove Myself

to endless bone scans,
PET scans,
nuclear scans.
Over and over
I had to drink
sweet icky
orange or pink
sticky stuff
that gave me
and others diarrhea.

Close to the waiting room
the bathroom stank.
The chairs were
hard. My back hurt.
It was easier to stand;
but then I got
in the way
of other unknowns
rushing back and forth.
Down in radiology
an hour seemed a day.

I pity all the caged
laboratory animals, I say.

Later the surgeon saw me
in ambulatory care.
He had to tell me
he could not operate
on my lung. It had to wait.
I needed chemotherapy

because I had more trouble
in my bones and blood.

Did you know that the left lung
has two lobes,
but the right one has three?
Or if two thirds of this
must be cut out
the other part will expand
to do the job? I did not
realize this then, but I do now.

Fall Flowers

James I. Stockwell

Blood Test

Am I anemic?
Do I have more
white cells
than red?

I'm meant to call
on Wednesday
for the results;

but the technician
to speak to
isn't there.

She'll phone
me tomorrow
and leave a message
if I'm gone.

Meanwhile
another's shuffling
through her papers.

"Hang on," she says.
"Yes, here it is, set aside.
Something seems

just a bit out of whack,
but it's not serious."

I respond to myself
hanging up,
"at least not
to the eyes of an oncologist."

Moving on into Morning

What was
is no more.
The window's black.
The moon is gone.
>Leaves fall
>to sea and dust.
>Bare trees bear up
>the wheeling stars.
Down the road
a piece, a dog barks
at what we know not.
>The X-ray you read
>shows a mass
>in my right lung.

After Admitting,
the waiting room is navy.
Next I drop my clothes.
The operating theater's
cold, windowless
white and stainless steel.
>The surgical folks
>are clad in cerulean.
>I peer around.
I am the only one not masked
and gloved. I am a stranger here:
Frost's trespasser asking
>for a glass of water.
>Then suddenly, snip-snap,
>I'm blacked out.

Waking, in Recovery
I wonder. What makes me
more than a name and number,
>prisoner of sorts
>till the snapped on
>paper bracelet's
>clipped off?

15

James I. Stockwell

October's the best month.
Cool and clear and fresh
unless the west wind blows
     coal smoke
     from Ohio.
     I breath it in
     `like leaf dust.
     What's the cause
     of this mass in my lungs?
October's the best month.

Tree Line

Waiting

By October
the smell of my own perfume
took my breath away.

And when my husband
laid a fire
and lit it against the cold

I had to close
The door and stay
in a far different room.

The day the X-ray was taken
I was told that it revealed
a suspicious looking nodule.

Soon a CT scan
showed two masses
in my right lung.

A diagnosis was needed,
so the next step was a bronchoscope
with anaesthesia to ease my fear.

The surgeon went through my nose.
I don't remember the rest,
just coughing up stuff.

When I woke in a few minutes,
it was enough. I was told
I had lung cancer.

How could that be? I hadn't smoked
in over forty years, and seldom before
except with coffee.

Well at least now I know
what's wrong with me,
which is kind of a relief.

Season Ending

Diagnosis

Spit, spot!
How come
there's blood
on my napkin?
Minuscule drops
      (but from
        where? tongue,
        lip or nostril?)
cause my heart
to leap up
and sink.
        What, oh what,
        dear one,
        could possibly
be the problem?

A foreign body
made up of
multiple
invisibles:
        particles
        of dust
        and silver fillings,
maybe. Say "ah"
says the humble
but persistent
doctor.
        "Get your lungs
        pictured
        fast as possible."

A nodule
looks suspicious,
so a CT scan's
ordered.
        It
shows a mass
in the right lung.

A bronchoscopy
follows and
    a biopsy's
      achieved.
   More scans reveal
   the cancer's
spread to hips,
    spine and ribs.

Mums

What's Happening?

I was relieved
to learn that people
can live for years and years
with just
one lung.
      For some reason
      the unexpected result
      of all my endless tests
      struck a funny
      bone.
Someone had an operation
scheduled in advance,
but now someone else
has had to cancel it
and talk about chemo first.

How come?
To see if the metastasis
will leave my blood and bones.
Otherwise there'll be
no need for further hurts.
      I'm but a babe in the woods
      as far as cancer's concerned.
      So I need to call up
      my sixteen-months-younger brother.
      He knows the ropes.
He's been fighting prostate cancer
for ten years plus.
He chose the knife
and it worked:
fought incontinence with grit and won.

Still sometimes his blood count leaps.
It's the aggressive kind
for which he has to take
testosterone lessening
pills from time to time.
      "Joe, I need your advice.

I'm dragging my heels about chemo.
I'm all for the quality of life.
Sometimes the trite cure
is worse than the disease."
Joe agrees. "Get a second opinion
first," he says, "before you decide.
Call it a consult
and always take Jimmy
with you to hear what you might miss."

Talking Long Distance

Joe says, "Make a list of questions
for your consult."
"I already have,
but what do you think
I should ask?"
     "First and foremost,
     what type of lung cancer
     do you have? And what stage is it?"
     Of course, these are important,
     but they weren't on my list
simply because I didn't know
enough to know there was a difference.
I've already been given a life span
of six months to three years
if I do nothing.

Close Hauled

Chapter 3: Second Opinion

After Hanging Up

I chose to call Dana-Farber's
thoracic unit on the eleventh floor
for a consult. If I want a second
       opinion I have to do a lot of work.
I have to ask those at the Baptist
       to send over my lab slides and notes
       and give me all my films
       to take with me when I go.
       This is not as easy as it might be.
       It involves a lot of phone calls.
Sometimes they don't have the copies ready.
I am tired and in pain, but I have to wait,
remembering that I meant business to that hospital;
and doctors like to refer patients
to their friends who work there.

It wasn't easy to get an appointment
at the new place either, but at last
it's Monday at one. I hate to have to take
the elevator here. At the Baptist
I could still climb the stairs;
       but I have a husband who doesn't mind
       punching buttons and holding my hand
       when I'm scared. He says he's willing
       to drive me to this high-rise
       if I chose its care.
It's taken a month to arrive.
I might have died by now but have not.
My films and lab reports have been read.
The Baptist's diagnosis is confirmed.
I have fourth stage common lung cancer
which has spread to bone and blood.

James I. Stockwell

What Can I Do?

Choose, choose!
The doctors leave
it all up to you.

The tests say
your cancer's
not contained.

When they get through
testing your body
it is covered

with sheets of papers
and information
you don't understand.

How could you?
Why should you?
You are the patient.

But the doctors
are afraid
of being sued.

Chemo, surgery,
or radiation implants,
which should you do?

The cancer's aggressive.
You have a 75 percent chance
of being cured.

I look at my left hand.
It has lost
its fingers

to the clenched fist
of a balled up
white-knuckled moon.

Geraniums

Plain Speaking

Today I have to decide
whether to receive
chemotherapy and fight

or let fourth stage
lung cancer steal
my quality of life.

What if I
lose my hair, my strength
and dignity
of mind?

What would a year
or two or three
give me if I'm all tied
up and miserable inside?

First Iris

The Choice is Mine to Make

Decide, decide,
choosing's hard.
At the Baptist it's easier
to park and far more familiar
to my mind.
      But Dana-Farber's
      all cancer
      and that is what
      I have. Here I am
      but one of thousands
who share
the same problems.
So how can I feel sorry
for myself or isolated
in such a crowd?

Misery loves company
I've found.
      To ward off cancer
      is a lifelong
      fight. I think I'll choose
      to try it here. My next
      appointment's in a week.
I'm told I qualify for the trial
drug, Tarceva. Its side effects
are often acne and diarrhea,
or sudden serious loss of breath;
but what have I got to lose?

To be in the trial one has to be over seventy years of age,
free of diabetes, and never had chemotherapy.
Am I lucky, or what? Tarceva's in its last
year of testing before it's expected to be
approved by the Food and Drug Administration.
      To stay in the program I'll have to take
      one chemo pill at home with a glass of water
      each morning on an empty stomach,
      at least an hour before breakfast.

Also I must keep a one line diary

of date and time taken and side effects.
And then come back every twenty-eight days
to draw a few vertical lines through horizontal graphs
documenting my quality of life;
and then get a harmless infusion of Zometa to strengthen
my bones before heading home with a month's supply of Tarceva.

Chapter 4: Beginning Treatment

At the Hospital

The man has a bunch
of fresh-scented
zinnias wrapped
in a wet newspaper
and clenched in his fist

for Matty who is black
and beautiful as a half-
moon's pregnant
sailing ship.
Still he loves her

though she has a belly full
of cancer
and turns away from him
with a fluttering
pink-palmed hand.

She becomes a butterfly
heading for South America
over rivers
and grasslands.
Yes,

this is how she will leave him,
just standing there
with his gift of zinnias
dripping
like a rainbow.

Last Blooms

Daily Rituals

Wake from rem sleep.
Take a chemo pill,
Tarceva, a molecule;
but of what? Swallow
it whole with lots
      of water. Leave
      no teeth marks.
Daydream for at least
an hour before eating
breakfast. Scribble
      a little poem
      from the heart.
Take a fresh breath in.
Let your own wastes go.

Start again. Eat
      a healthy hearty breakfast:
      braids of wheat.
      Smell the sea's
      salt scent. See
how albescent light appears
to rise like a salmon rose
out of that deep, flat green
      horizon to the east
when earth turns her back.
      Watch it ring
and climb tall trees
wound with knots of wind
      and minnowed mists
tickling tidal grass.

How suddenly
      a bloody
      sky becomes
      a bleeding
cloud of dust
under childhood's
      knuckle-boned moon:

no whole communion
wafer now. Just
      a chewed big C
for cancer's relief:
the fight in me
        sinking
down into the sea.

Namequoit River Inlet

After Chemo Pills

I itch,
I scratch,
and lift lidded
lashes
    till
    I pass
into the hills
of valleys
vanishing with
the blackness
of a licorice
waxing
crow flickering
candle.

Coming and Going

43

Chapter 5: Life with Tarceva

Ship to Shore Again

I'm really quite well,
     considering my options.
     A little sea-swell
of lung and belly
     makes me feel three months pregnant
     with an alien
quite foreign body.
     Lung cancer's my enemy
     to fight with bells on.
If this medicine
     doesn't work, my doctor tells
     me he's got plenty
of other drugs left
     to test that might accomplish
     life's desired ends.

Out to Sea

Waking

I say this sure is one
beautiful February day!
Look around you, dear
heart. As this blue planet
earth turns round, see
       how the sun
appears to rise to the east
out of Massachusetts Bay
like a valentine laced
with snow, clouds breaking
down as flotillas of ice cakes,
       flowering bare trees,
casting still barred shades
back into the tide's swing-swung,
       wave-spraying sea.

Suddenly everything's a flux
of motion like breathing in:
    filling up
    just to empty
    out both lungs,
the wings of my only heart
now with this double beat.
What does it mean, little one,
        when no wind's leaf
        stirs a swany star
   and all I know is nothing
   here on the brink of hard arms
   that won't let me sleep
      with my love?

   Look down again into the bay
   and glimpse yourself
   peering up. Crane up
   till nothing else
   seems to matter but
   the tip-tops of
   tall pines, impaling

dawn's pale yellow haze
like body fat: the weight
that light has left
behind as empty space,
filled with sea swells,
masses defining the dusts
of blood cells
that must adapt to change.

Sixth Sunday of Epiphany

While the minister is speaking
I am peering up at trees,
mostly majestic pines
reaching for the sky.

How come the pews are just
about as uncomfortable
as they can be?

Why am I here
on such a beautiful day?
My spine is aching

and my husband
can't take communion
at the kneeling rail
'cause he can't bend his knees.

I came for comfort.
I like to sing the hymns
and I want
to learn to pray.

I am lucky.
There are others here
far worse off than I.

And it's trite, but true,
that misery loves company.
Who said never take
a blind person's hand?

Close your eyes.
Let me take your arm
and follow as you guide.

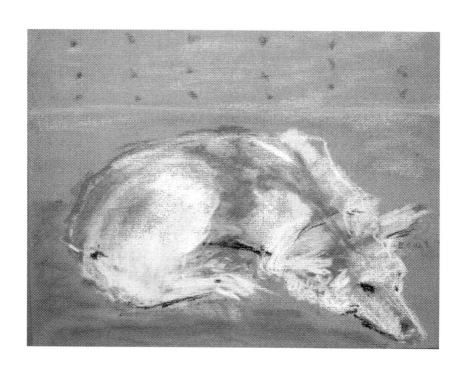

Snowflake at Rest

Chapter 6: Unknown Time Lines

How Come?

This taste of tin:
blistered tongue
and lip.
What have I done
to deserve this
punishment?
My ankles itch
       and swell upupup.
       My right rib
       aches for love.
But the skin on my face is
a red chenille spread, covered
with a trillion little
white-headed pimples.

Every once
in a while symptoms
such as these vanish
like a lucky
gift;
and then just as suddenly
flare up
again with persistence,
but never all at once
 as if I'd been sitting
in summer sun
sizzling
unaware
till overdone.

James I. Stockwell

An Orange Alert

Tarceva's my friend.
She tried to help me and did.
    But good things must end.
Little problems too:
    nerve endings wound with arched ribs
    cling to barred heart strings.
Water sloshes at
    the bottom of my right lung.
    My craft is sinking.
I am scared to swim
    with dolphins. But my life vest
    blinks bright as a star
easily glimpsed at night.
    But who can see me bobbing
    in the blinding light?

Downwind

James I. Stockwell

Just Waking Up

Taste of tin.
Taste of sawdust
in the wind.
> Blinkers
> full of
> grit.
Skin
rubbed red
and pimpled.
> Cuticles
> blundering,
> blistered.
Nothing is
as it was
before this
> thinning
> of once
> thick
bright hair. So still
the biggest question
lingers in late April
> mist.
> How come
> I will
persist with
the daily drug,
this little
> chemo pill?
> How long do I want
> to live?

Waterfall

What is Left to Lose?

Quality of life's
       the gift Tarceva gave me.
       And heart's more grateful
than mind can say for
       six months of great energy
       and amazing health.
But now I'm barely
       hanging on to a split craft.
       My savior wants me
to take Taxol: blood
       of old growth northwestern yews.
       But such tapped off saps
might close up my throat
       as diphtheria's strength did
       to my Uncle Taddy.

Winter Hill

Chapter 7: Taxol and Carboplatin

Losing Energy

Two weeks following
the biggest chemo treatment,
Taxol and Carboplatin
plus steroids and Benadryl
to help side effects,
my red cell counts drop,
as is expected;
so I get a shot
and am told it would be
good to eat red meat.
Mostly, I'm a vegetarian,
but the best of rules are made
to break, and so I guess
I'll indulge childhood's craving
for roast beef and steak.

Risking Everything

Taste of tin,
taste of sawdust,
blood on lower lip
and tongue,
scent of a strip-
mine plus
old growth timbers
cut. Disastrous!
Nothing is as it
was before us.
Plain bread with-
out salt tastes of
dust, but still
beats swelling up.

Thawing

These days more
new moon hairs
catch in my comb;
    and more
        chipped nails
        keep falling
        like snow
to soft fir floors,
till all that keeps on
living, after air
    and water
        turn to stone,
appears to be going,
gone, gone.
Who knows where?

Spring Melt

Silent Dialogue

You have already
taken a reading
of my heart.

It's got a steady
metronome beat
like the sea.

So, what's left
for us to do together
doctor?

I am better.
You are pleased
and I've got to get

something completed
which makes it easier
to leave.

It's hot
in this blue exam room.
My heart's
a melting ruby
splotched
with dew stupid
as a star.
So what else is new?
It's hard.
What did you say, Rumi?
It does not
matter?
Ah,
but to whom?

James I. Stockwell

Just Farewell

After Carboplatin
chemo I've got
better breath
and no swollen legs;
but what if I get
on a jet plane
to fly coast to coast
and see Cassidy
graduate, and nod off
or bleed from a vein
when I applaud
'cause my blood
counts and platelets
are too low?

Sound Asleep

Chapter 8: Keeping Up a Good Front

Who?

You who have no voice
to phone,
no hand or word
to write a letter,
are you mine?

You who own no coat
to share or shed
as snowflakes
on the earth
and in the air,

you who have no feet
to bear my weight
the extra mile,
are you alone forever?

You who have no size
that I can measure
have taken me
to bed again
for pleasure.

With the temperature
of light drops of oil
you give me wings:
the terror of your leisure.

You have stolen
all my choices

and desires,
like a virus
or a lover.

Who Knows?

Tonight I might
ask you
to rub my back
counterclockwise.

Time is relative
but light
is absolute.

And so perhaps it's life
that lets us stand
in the shadows,

and death
that flies
beyond the stones
as we dance.

Snowflake and Crystal

Scent of Sap

Taste of tin,
    taste of sawdust
in the wind
with fumbling
fingers,
    one must
stand still
and let go of
Tarceva's kid
with dusty
    fluid
wings, and trust
the singing.

Love's lungs and belly
    ache a bit
    and swell.
It's as if I were six
months pregnant,
but without the kick.
I'm not myself.
I've got no little
one tongued bell
    to ring
for universal help
above the winging
flood except myself
    tinkling.

All I know
is I'm scared
to stay home
on a quaking threshold.
Oh, who can bear it?
My advice to those
who sooner or later

might need chemo
is let your hair
grow.

Let it hang
like Spanish moss
in an old growth
rain forest
as long as you can.
Let it blow
with the wind's last
sea coasting
blast of breath
and sacred estuary
waters below it.

Full Bloom

James I. Stockwell

Late Chemo Results

A CT scan shows
the mass in my lung
is breaking up.

I picture a bumping
crowd of folks
leaving a Catholic church

where I'm still
sitting just wondering
how come
they're going.

Are they heading
home or maybe
to the graveyard
for a burial?

Chemo-Infusion

Molecules of bark
 from a dark northwestern yew
  enter me in drops.

The purpose being what:
 to help the body's cells stop,
  as brave warriors

to fight swift divides
 like rivers multiplying
  springs past wintertime?

I am so tired
 of pollen's antique golden gods
  that keep following

me like tomorrow.
 Three times Death's said, not good-bye,
  but farewell my child.

Oh my dearest heart,
 when will it be time to stop
  and fly with wild swans?

James I. Stockwell

Out of Control

Foot to the floor,
my husband careens his car
down the hill.
His brakes attempt to grab
but can't hold on.
     His knees won't bend
     but his stubborn heart
     got a pacemaker implant.
     He's no more or less
     than a "bionic man"
with a wear-worn
bald spot who has not
ever known how to stop.
Frost's "harness gall"
is what I call it.

As for me, my head's
turban wound after
chemo 'cause my dirty blond
hair's all gone: puffed
off as cloudy lungs.
     Now all my tongue
     can taste is tin
     and sawdust stars
     in such a sudden
     strip-mined wind.
What else in the dark is
there for us to wish for
following such a crash,
'cept blood's present touch:
self's rush for the other love?

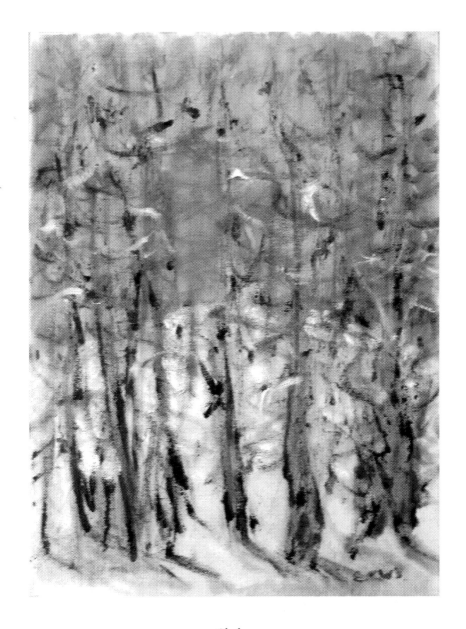

Shelter

James I. Stockwell

After Chemotherapy

Everybody's different.
For instance, I've got
fuzzy feet
like felt slippers;
and foggy
            eyes awash
as if within the sea's
channel chop.
            I wish
I had New Balance sneakers
with good arches
to support the twins
that still live here within
this hardly beating heart;
but I do not.

These days most grains
taste like sawdust from a tin;
most food, in fact,
except for beautiful fruit
and charbroiled steak
which is cruel.
            Lately
I walk stiff-legged as if
back in childhood's shoes
and often lose
my balance,
            barefoot,
as the wind
that slips through cracks
invites confusion.

Now I'm bald
as a baby.
My brown hair's gone.
            What's left is grey

and wispy.
Bare and ashamed,
I wear a cap.

Still my fingernails
are pitted.
All that keeps on
living after
death appears to have lost
it's shimmer;
but it will come back
I'm told by my doctor.

Reaching Up

Wig On

My head
is bald,
she said,
as a newborn's.

Unsteady,
old and worn,
I'm ready
to move on.

Every breath's
an effort.

So don't talk,
just listen
to the song
of the wren:

no thought
of death

just the loss
of egg and nest
all gone in the fall,
but remembered.

Who Ever Knows?

The first gold
tree's a cherry.
The sky's cerise and mauve.
The grass is green.
The fog unscrolls
like Great Blue Herons.
Sparrows, like brown leaves,
drop to dust and stones.
Laughing Gulls scream
and the sea's grief
is my own.
Oh why do I keep wondering
when the time comes
will I be ready to go?

Still I keep walking
in shore grass
where the shadows
of falling
leaves dance
with sparrows.

And the laughter
of children is my own.

Tonight my dream's
a pair of pinching shoes
I can't wait to
kick off so I can
swim with you
south of the border.

Chapter 9: Terminating Chemotherapy

Over and Over

I walk here alone
  on a path of flattened straws
   and round, tripping stones

the ocean has rolled
  back and forth like stupid songs.
   I walk here alone

scaring off three crows.
  The dead have walked here before
   tripping on these stones

and never gone home.
  You have driven to Boston.
   So I walk alone

crunching shells and bones.
  The sea doesn't know you're gone.
   It keeps skipping stones.

Sun and sea roses
  reflect blood in the water.
   I walk here alone

with my own shadow
  and form darkening earth's door.
   I walk here alone,
    clouds dripping on stone.

These Days after Chemo

Here by an oyster colored bay
I feel as if I'm being poisoned.
Beauty lives in the shadows.
        But where is joy
when only faithful sorrow
stays, and wheeling pain creates
        splitting rainbows?

I am recalling "Arsenic and Old Lace."
Our frayed rose-tweed couch posed
        for recycled flight takes off
and lands upside down
on our living room's white ceiling;
but now it's quite different:
        I'm the fade-out spinning.

I no longer want to see the sea.
Its' back and forth is all
too sheepdog restless for me,
        though it will be
here so long after I have gone,
gnashing soft teeth across
        a broad green lawn.

I have no more time for passion
or extreme beauty's cruelty
flickering on the brink of more
        than can be perceived:
fallen leaves: black throated sparrows
caught in gutters. I am exhausted.
        All I want is peace.

Sails at Rest

Husband and Wife

What you like to do
    I do not.
And yet I think
    I understand
what makes you tick.

You were the loner in our youth,
and I the "groupie."
But now that time
    is running out
I wonder: have we two

become the opposite sides
of one another's moods,
    even as the tide
turns counterclockwise
to the wind and moon?

Spine to spine we lie,
    he and I,
    his heat
radiating into me as mine.

He says, "Your face is white.
    Do you feel okay?"
    "A little shaky

    and bleedy
still from the operation,
the procedure," I reply.

Ah, so this is the way
he gives her comfort
when back to back two face
    each other.

Resting

Yesterday I stepped outside
and breathed in
ninety degrees of thick pollution's
sticky heat.
     So then when I climbed
     steep steps to lie
     down for a while,
I grew dizzy with sea legs
and had to hang onto the rail
for dear life's
balance. As if on a ship,
my eyes swam as when lifted
with the bends
from a deep, deep dive.

Then when
I hit bottom
I had to wrestle
a shy squid
     till the ink
     in my pen was his
     blood in my veins
and I became a cold
creature scribbling
like the east wind,
     not knowing what
     it was doing,
     and caring less
till it got a poem.

After that I woke
from my wake
with nothing
to say
     'cause I was dead
     of heart and mind;
     and soul was something
     I couldn't explain

though the light
shone plain and simple
             as a ring of gold
             on a banded Eider's
reptilian leg.

Summer Scene

Chapter 10: Rough Water

What's Wrong?

I'm dizzy   as a dervish.
Is it just   exhaustion
or something   more?

Spinning as spun   by white water
under dim   starry orbs
I seesaw   by a seashore

till   red leaves flicker-
fall   by silver water,
oblivious   to wind.

As blood drips   from war
and Thor's   thunder splits
dusk from dawn   before

I   step indoors
and hear it   whistle
as I bounce wall   to wall.

In this narrow unlit   hall
I slip   invisible
as a snake's skin   on

a soft   carpet of colors
unable to wave   so long
to DNA's   amazing glory.

Always here,   never gone
One   keeps   trying to hang on
where brittle   leaves litter

James I. Stockwell

earth until I glimpse   myself in
silver water's   mirror,
where I walk   snip-

snap like scissors,   as nothing
but a stitch   in the worn fabric
of life's strong   stretched cloth.

Iris Dance

Sunday Morning

Outside in our dogs' fenced yard
last night's heat has cooled.
I look to starred trees
and praise their sibling blue
      and pale cadmium green
      genuflecting leaves
      fanning fresh air free
      of a recent rain's dews.
This that you and I breathe in
to survive and expel human
wastes from purple veins
is what trees need and receive
from us in exchange, to bloom
and provide sweet summer shade.

When you say, "absolutely,"
what do you really mean?
Is the tide really
as high as it can be?
Have you ever experienced
the celadon sky of a typhoon
or the jaundiced skin
of a newborn child
trembling on cold scales?
Is not a pain increased
by what it indicates?
Please don't ask me
to give pain a number, a degree.
At least to me everything seems
relative, as time to light's speed.

A mere sprained ankle once caused
a rainbow in my brain to wheel me floor
to ceiling. I dragged myself indoors
and lay stretched flat out
on our old pink tweed couch.
March ground's freeze and thaw
and creep and crawl caught

my halting left foot, as I walked
and turned to stop and look up
at a Nuthatch rushing upside down
a tree trunk, sky to ground
And so it still is as it was.
I am just a little dizzy, that's all,
at least until the next inexorable fall.

Snowflake

Out of the Blue

Last night
was hard.
Every hour
or two I got
       a sharp cramp
       that might
be a clot.
So I stood
up fast,
       walked around
       and sank
       back down
as a swimmer
in the swallowing dark.

Chapter 11: Who's in Charge?

Far from Heaven

Who knows what's next?
    Though death
is almost always expected
    don't we all tend
to quite completely forget
    to remember ends.
Periods are where the next sentence
    starts each letter
in the right or wrong direction:
    at least a step
until we trip the light fantastic, yes
    and find ourselves
slipping dizzily down hill on wet
    leaves and snow melt:
the sound of sleigh bells
    wound with rain pelt,
and peepers on the brink of lent:
    the memory
of sweets given up: Ash Wednesday's
    spring retreat: the smell
of skunks: the seasick swell:
    life's tenancy:
the big C a brand new moon presents:
    cancer in the cells!
Gravity's disease! The very day you fell
    was the day you met
the young man, Jesus, by the well:
    not yet risen
Christ, not God's embodiment,
    but far less,
no star before the more that lets
    us all get

James I. Stockwell

up from transubstantiation's depths
    to glimpse the errors
of our ways and begin again
    with fear and trembling
as the wings of angels press
    and descend
through the ever increasing darkness
    of velleity's sedges:
breath's clearing albescence.

Late Afternoon

Death Wish

Blue skies. Windows wide. No place to hide.
Too far to fly: a grey-white dream realized!

Agoraphobia sets in. West wind   unsettles things.
Earth's axis,   birth's stasis   tips and spins.

The road is white.   Springside snow is white.   When I was a child,
afraid to sing,   the prevailing wind   gave me wings,

or stopped me still   at the top   of Heartbreak Hill.
Decide. Decide.   Keep on climbing   and falling ad infinitum

or give up   gravity's ambition. The choice is mine.

To Survive

My doctor says
we have to fight
nature.
        Ah, yes;
but the question is:
how long do I want
to live?
        At what
cost longevity:
forgetful,
        songless
loss of pride,
sweet dignity
and warm desire.

Chapter 12: Meeting of Minds

Belief

When I'm gone
how will you
remember me?
Like a song?
A drop of dew?
A leaf?

A hilly dawn
staying here with blue
veined feet?
Mean tide crossed
by a light wave
I can not see?

A small tossing
of salad greens?
All gone
as childhood cookies
in a jar of dreams?

Gravity's loss?
One egg and seed
becoming a unique
human being
walking beneath
a willow tree?

James I. Stockwell

Scent of salt?
 A little mutable
 edema?
 Ooze
of estuary
streams?

Night lights snapped on
 shy as two soft shoes
  so as not to see
  the moon
 but hear
the sea?

Estuary

James I. Stockwell

As a Blue Wind Blows

Low to high
and high to low
the mean tide
comes and goes.
From brinks of time
in different globe-
zones midnight's
poppies dance and glow
          as firelight
          casting shadows
          to your grave site.
Love of life
I must soon let you go
without a fight.

Chapter 13: Tight Quarters

These Days

Nothing much tastes good.
Sometimes I find it hard
to remember who I am
or who you are.
In a cool, leafy wood
a Snowy Owl who whos
and blinks its two
eyes like Jupiter's moons,
night to day: wide awake
and then good-bye.
I am so tired.
All I want to do
is drift away
back to sleep in time.

Fogged In

Figuring Things Out

We are all born mad.
Some remain so.
—Bertolt Brecht, *Waiting for Godot*

It's hard,
isn't it dear heart,
to be the spouse?
The aging patient
gets all the attention
at the hospital
and back home again.

The kids are gone,
but still you have
to do your job,
and shop for clothes
and food, and walk the dogs
and take care of more
than a dark house.

It's important
to take care
of yourself!

So ring
a few bells
and ask
for some help.

"The past
is a foreign country,"
As Pinter says.

So do what you love
or else
fall apart.

To and Fro

Cracked Mirror

My skin's a ruin.
  The sun has done his damage:
   red spots and ashes:
    constellations, Magellan
     clouds dancing on scrims of snow.

A wrinkled ocean
  wears a universal face.
   Aging takes courage
    and a place to go and stay
     before the party's over.

So while there's still time
  make end of life decisions
   and a tone poem
    flown from memory, those days
     another sets to music.

To use a baby boomer's vernacular: old
  age is a bummer.
   True! Unless fate is lucky
    and has a sense of humor.

So do what you want.
  Make something lovely come true.
   Whether old or young,
    the choosing of the best time
     to go must be up to you.

A Personal View

Darlene snaps on the ceiling light
and obliterates the moon.
She says it's cold outside.

It's hard to move.
I'm growing slight.
Will I improve?

When she goes, the night
turns slightly blue.
My sheets are white.

Josephine is black and beautiful.
She will take my vital signs
before she leaves the room.

She is also very kind.
This is no illusion.

Chapter 14: Final Weeks

Out of Sight

Close your eyes.
Breath deeply.
Somebody's dying.

Feel the light.
Hear the sea.
Close your eyes.

It's a blue night.
Let it be!
Somebody's dying.

The sky is white
as an Easter lily.
Close your eyes.

Let Spirit rise
like mist from freeze.
Somebody's dying,

wilting like a wild
flower in the street.
Close your eyes.
Who is dying?

Exhilaration

Green sky with a fringe
 of leaves tickles him and me
  here beside the sea.
   Little peaches on the tree
    of fall rinsed by rain splatter
mirror dappled streams,
 dimple-nippling light's skin
  where fishes surface
   lipping as if hinting at
    low inlets where a soul sleeps:
the way one might play
 a keyboard in a silent
  dream surpassing reason,
   like a tipping craft reefed in
    to slice through increasing waves.

Let the wind take me,
 I say. It doesn't matter.
  I'm sick anyhow.
   So what difference does it make
    if I drift with the current?
I'm shy; hate good-byes.
 I'd rather slip-slide away
  from all those I love
   towards some safe estuary,
    like a snowy Albatross
skimming ocean waves,
 wings outstretched, still practicing
  for perfect updrafts,
   alighting and vanishing.
    Oh, who knows where I'll land next?

Sunshine

Growing Smaller

Oh! What's this dance
of life all about?
Where is it taking us:
all this hanging on
and then letting go;
all this coming close
and stepping back
just to turn around
and maybe know
what love alone can't?
It hurts too much
unless one's glad
the dance is done.
Over with. Caput.

Chapter 15: Troubling Times

Is This the End?

We have not been here long,
less than the blink of an eye
or the single note of a song;

in geological time, a bleep so small
that as we see and then hear it fly,
though we have not been here long,

it is gone
dark as light
years before the single note of a song.

Are we important
mights,
though we have not been here long;

a drop of water,
a bird, a blip in time,
the single word of a song?

These are more than all our nights
though we have not been here long
we are a part of the song.

James I. Stockwell

Ashes to Ashes

Please don't scatter me
over the bay or seashore
where children love to play
in the dog lapping waves
and the water often appears
grated carrot colored
in the early morning.

Plant me instead by a healing
willowed and meandering stream,
where trout sleep like stone
and birdsong springs
from winter's deepest silence
and nothing we once believed
to be colorless and dead
really is.

Trees

Chapter 16: A Kiss Good-bye

Risking More

How can I tell
you what you've done
for me?

No tinkling bell,
no Bluebird singing from
a dew tipped tree,

no swelling
light-wave bent by dust,
no spraying sea,

no pelting
rain like ashen tongues
on genuflecting leaves,

no other's help
from deep above
or high beneath,

no white or red blood cells
suddenly sprung
free,

nothing, no one else
could ever do as much
as you have for me:

loves's swallowed self
that lets another
be!

Front Hall Flowers